Sports Illustrated KIDS

A SUPERFAN'S GUIDE TO
PRO Baseball TEAMS

By Drew Lyon

CAPSTONE PRESS
a capstone imprint

Sports Illustrated Kids Pro Sports Team Guides are published by Capstone Press, a Capstone Imprint, 1710 Roe Crest Drive, North Mankato, Minnesota 56003. www.capstonepub.com

Sports Illustrated Kids is a trademark of Time Inc. Used with permission.

Library of Congress Cataloging-in-Publication Data
is available on the Library of Congress website:
ISBN: 978-1-5157-8851-5 (library binding)
ISBN: 978-1-5157-8857-7 (eBook PDF)

Editorial Credits
Elizabeth Johnson and Nate LeBoutillier, editors; Terri Poburka, designer; Eric Gohl, media research; Gene Bentdahl, production specialist

Photo Credits
Dreamstime: Jerry Coli, 2m, 8l, 15r, 16l, 34r, 46r, 47l, Keeton10, 8r, Ron Hoff, 39l; Getty Images: Focus On Sport, 62l; Library of Congress: 5, 17r, 24l, 43r; Newscom: AI Wire Photo Service/Mike Yelman, 36l, Cal Sport Media/Joy Absalon, 61r, EPA/Tannen Maury, 42r, Icon SMI/TSN, 38l, Icon Sportswire/Cliff Welch, 50r, Icon Sportswire/Doug Murray, 26r, Icon Sportswire/Frank Jansky, cover (bottom), 17l, 43l, Icon Sportswire/Kevin French, 6r, 36r, Icon Sportswire/Matthew Pearce, 60r, Icon Sportswire/Patrick Gorski, 14r, Icon Sportswire/Scott W. Grau, 16r, Icon Sportswire/Steve Nurenberg, 55l, UPI/Pat Benic, 21l, 23l, ZUMA Press/Brian Peterson, 39r, ZUMA Press/Hayne Palmour IV, 51l, ZUMA Press/Malcolm W. Emmons, 10l, ZUMA Press/St Petersburg Times, 58l, ZUMA Press/Will Vragovic, 58r; Shutterstock: B Brown, cover (top), Chones, throughout (trophies), Debby Wong, 3m, 40r, 41l, Fabio Alcini, 68l, Keeton Gale, 9l, 20r, 27l, Marie C Fields, 4bl, Mega Pixel, throughout (pennant), Mike Flippo, throughout (vintage cleats), Naypong, throughout (vintage glove), O'Jay R. Barbee, 68–69m, 70–71, 72, Sean Locke Photography, 69br, Svetlana Larina, 69tr; Sports Illustrated: Al Tielemans, 2r, 3l, 10r, 12r, 19l, 44r, 48r, 49l, 54r, 57l, 62r, 63l, Andy Hayt, 25r, 26l, Bob Rosato, 35r, Chuck Solomon, 20l, 27r, Damian Strohmeyer, 55r, 59l, 59r, David E. Klutho, 18r, 29l, 33l, 35l, 37l, Heinz Kluetmeier, 6l, 29r, 37r, 41r, 45r, 47r, 48l, 64l, 65r, John Biever, 7l, 7r, 15l, 21r, 24r, 38r, John D. Hanlon, 44l, 57r, John G. Zimmerman, 13r, 33r, 42l, John Iacono, 30l, 40l, 46l, 50l, 51r, 54l, 60l, 63r, John W. McDonough, 31r, 61l, Lane Stewart, 12l, Mark Kauffman, 49r, 56l, Peter Read Miller, 23r, Richard Meek, 32l, 52l, Robert Beck, 2l, 3r, 11r, 13l, 22l, 22r, 25l, 28r, 30r, 31l, 32r, 34l, 45l, 52r, 53l, 53r, 56r, Simon Bruty, 11l, 64r, 65l, Tony Triolo, 14l, V.J. Lovero, 9r, Walter Iooss Jr., 18l, 19r, 28l

Design Elements: Shutterstock

All statistics have been updated through the 2016 MLB season.

Printed in Canada
10728R

TABLE OF CONTENTS

KNOW IT ALL

Ask a Yankees fan who batted cleanup for the 1961 team, and he'll tell you it was Mickey Mantle. Ask a Red Sox fan who was on the mound when the team won the 2004 World Series, and she'll tell you it was Keith Foulke. Ask a Dodgers fan what position Jackie Robinson played, and he'll tell you Robinson was a second baseman — and a good one at that.

Baseball fans are devoted to their favorite teams. They know all the players' names and faces and numbers. They've memorized the crucial dates and important records in the club's history. And they're loyal through bad times, always feeling sure things will be different next year. That's what it means to be a fan.

It's something else to be a superfan. What is the difference? Superfans want to know it all. They steep themselves in the stories and numbers that tell the story of Major League Baseball (MLB). They check the results of every game and track the standings all summer. They follow every team. They can't get enough.

Arizona
DIAMONDB

The Arizona Diamondbacks — often called the D-Backs — are one of Major League Baseball's newest teams. They were formed in 1998 and placed in the National League's West division. In the D-Backs' fourth season, hard-throwing pitchers Randy Johnson and Curt Schilling helped Arizona win the World Series. No other expansion team had captured a title so fast. The 2001 win was an epic upset over the mighty New York Yankees in a Game 7 comeback.

WON/LOSS RECORD:
1,503-1,575 (.488 W-L%)

HOME BASE:
Chase Field

SUPERFACT

Chase Field in Phoenix has air conditioning and a retractable roof to protect players and fans from heat and bad weather. Fans can also cool off by taking a dip in a pool that sits behind the right-center field wall.

Then & Now

RANDY JOHNSON 1999–2004; 2007–08 / ZACK GREINKE 2016–present

ACKS

TROPHY CASE

World Series Champions:
2001

World Series Co-MVPs:
**Randy Johnson and
Curt Schilling, 2001**

Franchise Leaders:
Single-season home run record:
Luis Gonzalez, 57 (2001)

Single-season strikeouts:
Randy Johnson, 372 (2001)

Single-season stolen bases:
Tony Womack, 72 (1999)

Single-season walks:
Paul Goldschmidt, 118 (2015)

SUPERFACT

Paul "Goldy" Goldschmidt worked hard to achieve baseball success and remained humble and polite even after he became a pro player. He is now a four-time All-Star and the founder of Goldy's Fund 4 Kids, a charity that raises money for children at the Phoenix Children's Hospital. Paul and his wife, Amy, host an annual bowling tournament and donate all the proceeds to his charity.

Atlanta
BRAVES

The Braves have resided in Atlanta since 1966, but their roots date back to 1871. The Braves are considered one of the oldest franchises in American professional sports. They are also the only franchise to win the World Series in three different cities—Boston (1914), Milwaukee (1957), and Atlanta (1995). From 1991 to 2005, the Braves were a dynasty, setting an MLB record by winning their division 14 years in a row.

WON/LOSS RECORD:
10,438-10,432 (.500 W-L%)

HOME BASE:
SunTrust Park

SUPERFACT

The Braves have worn the same white home uniforms since 1987. The team's gray road uniforms are a throwback to the jerseys worn when the Braves were based in Boston and Milwaukee.

Then & Now

HANK ARRON 1954–74 / ADONIS GARCIA 2015–present

TROPHY CASE

1914 (Boston), 1957 (Milwaukee)
1995 (Atlanta)

Franchise Leaders:

Career home runs:
Hank Aaron, 733

Career RBI:
Hank Aaron 2,202

Career wins:
Warren Spahn, 356

Single-season saves:
John Smoltz, 55 (2002)

Single-season ERA:
Greg Maddux, 1.56 (1994)

Single-season times on base:
Chipper Jones, 309 (1999)

SUPERFACT

Atlanta pitcher **Julio Teheran** is only one of two Colombian-born players in MLB history to reach the All-Star game. Teheran had a passion for soccer when he was younger, but that changed when his uncle, a Braves scout, gave him his first ball glove. Teheran was signed by the Braves at the age of 16.

Baltimore
ORIOLES

The Baltimore Orioles were established in 1954—they were formerly the St. Louis Browns—and are in the American League's East division. They've won three World Series, and were in the playoffs as recently as 2016. Baltimore legend Cal Ripken set a baseball record when he played in 2,632 games in a row from May 1982 until September 1998.

WON/LOSS RECORD:
8,592-9,418 (.477 W-L%)

HOME BASE:
Camden Yards

SUPERFACT

The Orioles uniform features the team name in a classic cursive font across the chest. In 2012 the O's brought back the cartoon oriole cap that Baltimore players first wore from 1966–1988. The cartoon bird is also the team's mascot, named the Oriole Bird, of course.

Then & Now
FRANK ROBINSON 1966–71 / ADAM JONES 2008–present

SUPERFACT

Manny Machado was drafted by the Orioles after his senior year of high school. His grandfather taught him the fundamentals of baseball when Manny was growing up in southern Florida. Machado made his major league debut just a few months after his 20th birthday in 2012. Many fans consider Machado to be the most talented Oriole since Cal Ripken. In 2016 Machado hit three grand slams, tying the MLB record for slams in a season by a player aged 24 or younger.

TROPHY CASE

World Series Champions:
1966, 1970, 1983

Franchise Leaders:
Consecutive games played:
Cal Ripken, 2,632 (MLB record)

Career hits: **Cal Ripken, 3,184**

Single-season batting average:
George Sisler, .420 (1922)

Single-season home runs:
Chris Davis, 53 (2013)

Boston
RED SOX

The Red Sox are one of baseball's most popular teams. After an 86-year title drought, they broke the "Curse of the Bambino" and became the first baseball team to come back from a 3-0 series deficit in 2004. Happily for Sox fans, this accomplishment came againts their archrivals, the New York Yankees, to take the American League pennant. They went on to win the World Series and also added titles in 2007 and 2013.

WON/LOSS RECORD:
9,317-8,707 (.517 W-L%)

HOME BASE:
Fenway Park

SUPERFACT

The Red Sox have featured the same red and white uniform and logo since 1946. When Boston plays on St. Patrick's Day during spring training, the team dons green jerseys in tribute to the city of Boston's Irish heritage.

Then & Now

CARL YASTRZEMSKI 1961–83 / DUSTIN PEDROIA 2006-present

World Series Champions:
1903, 1912, 1915, 1916,
1918, 2004, 2007, 2013

Franchise Leaders:

Single-season hits:
Wade Boggs, 240 (1985)

Single-season home runs:
David Ortiz, 54 (2006)

Single-season strikeouts:
Pedro Martinez, 313 (1999)

Single-game stolen bases:
Jacoby Ellsbury, 5

Career batting average:
Ted Williams, .344

Career games played:
Carl Yastrzemski, 3,308

Career triples:
Harry Hooper, 130

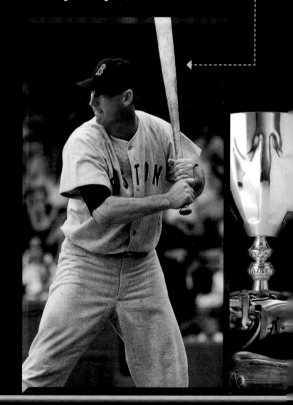

SUPERFACT

Red Sox shortstop **Xander Bogaerts**
may have the coolest nickname in
baseball. The "X-Man" won a World
Series in his rookie year in 2013,
becoming the third-youngest player in
baseball history to hit a triple in the
Series. The All-Star is only the fifth
player from the country of Aruba to
reach the big leagues. The X-Man can
also speak four languages.

Chicago CUBS

The Cubs have often been called "the lovable losers." That all changed in 2016, when the Cubs finally achieved the unthinkable: winning their first World Series in 108 years. The Cubs battled back from a 3-1 series deficit to force a Game 7 in Cleveland versus the Indians. In an instant classic, Chicago defeated Cleveland, 8-7, in 10 innings.

WON/LOSS RECORD:
10,711-10,188 (.513 W-L%)

HOME BASE:
Wrigley Field

SUPERFACT

Since the late 1960s, the Cubs have kept a similar home uniform: classic pinstripes adorned with the team's logo on the left shoulder. Throughout the team's history, there have been nine different bear logos on its jerseys.

Then & Now

IVAN DE JESUS 1977–81 / KRIS BRYANT 2015–present

SUPERFACT

Anthony Rizzo struggled in his rookie season with the San Diego Padres and was subsequently traded to Chicago. But the trade was hardly the biggest shakeup of his life. Diagnosed with Hodgkin's lymphoma in 2008, Rizzo underwent chemotherapy. The treatment was successful, and Rizzo went on to blossom with the Cubs. He is now the founder of a non profit organization that helps the families of those battling cancer.

TROPHY CASE

World Series Champions:
1907, 1908, 2016

Franchise Leaders:

Single-season strikeouts:
Bill Hutchinson, 314 (1892)

Single-season home runs:
Sammy Sosa, 66 (1998)

Single-season stolen bases:
Bill Lange, 84 (1896)

Single-season hits:
Rogers Hornsby, 229 (1929)

Most Gold Gloves:
Ryne Sandberg, 9

Chicago
WHITE SOX

In 2005 the Chicago White Sox started an unlikely run, bringing the first World Series title back to the city's South Side since 1917. Founded in 1901, the White Sox have been one of the league's most well-known franchises even if they weren't always a winning ball club. The 2005 team was led by Paul Konerko, A.J. Pierzynski, Jermaine Dye, and Mark Buehrle.

WON/LOSS RECORD:
9,082-8,931 (.504 W-L%)

HOME BASE:
Guaranteed Rate Field

SUPERFACT

The White Sox sport one of baseball's most enduring logos, the word "Sox" spelled in an English font. In 1960 they were the first pro sports franchise to place their players' last names on the back of the jerseys.

Then & Now
TOM SEAVER 1984—86 / JOSE QUINTANA 2012-present

SUPERFACT

White Sox first baseman **Jose Abreu** fled Cuba in 2013 to play in the big leagues. A year later he was named the American League's Rookie of the Year. When he made the 2014 All-Star game, it marked the first time his parents saw their son play in the big leagues. At the beginning of his pro career, Jose's mother told him to pick a high uniform number — 79 — so people would remember him. Mission accomplished!

TROPHY CASE

World Series Champions:
1906, 1917, 2005

World Series MVP:
Jermaine Dye (2005)

Franchise Leaders:
Single-season home runs:
Albert Belle, 49 (1998)

Single-season batting average:
Luke Appling, .388 (1936)

Single-season saves:
Bobby Thigpen, 57 (1990)

Career batting average:
Shoeless Joe Jackson, .340

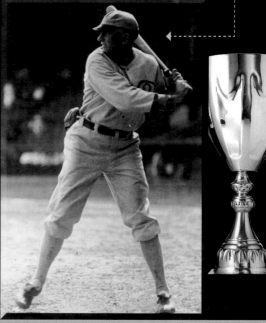

Cincinnati REDS

The Cincinnati Red Stockings (later shortened to "Reds") were established in 1882 and joined the National League in 1890. They've won five World Series, most notably during the "Big Red Machine" dynasty of the 1970s. Thirty-one Reds players have been enshrined in the National Baseball Hall of Fame.

WON/LOSS RECORD:
10,389-10,117 (.507 W-L%)

HOME BASE:
Great American Ball Park

SUPERFACT

In 1956 the Reds became only the second franchise to use sleeveless jerseys. In the 1990s the team re-introduced the sleeveless jerseys but dropped them in 2000 after undergoing another uniform change.

Then & Now

JOHNNY BENCH 1967–83 / BILLY HAMILTON 2013–present

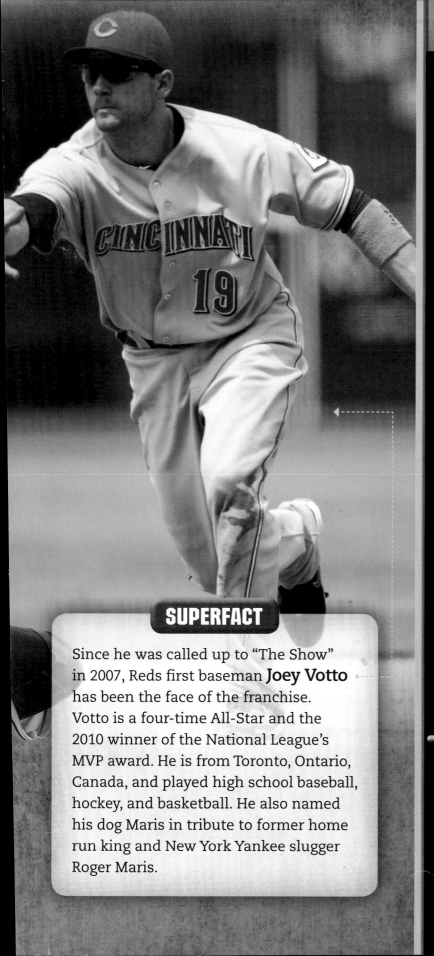

TROPHY CASE

World Series Champions:
World Series Champions:
1919, 1940, 1975, 1976, 1990

Franchise Leaders:

Single-season home runs:
George Foster, 52 (1977)

Single-season bases on balls:
Joey Votto, 143 (2015)

Games played:
Pete Rose, 2,722

Career hits:
Pete Rose, 3,358

Career RBI:
Johnny Bench, 1,376

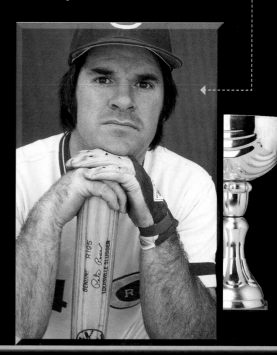

SUPERFACT

Since he was called up to "The Show" in 2007, Reds first baseman **Joey Votto** has been the face of the franchise. Votto is a four-time All-Star and the 2010 winner of the National League's MVP award. He is from Toronto, Ontario, Canada, and played high school baseball, hockey, and basketball. He also named his dog Maris in tribute to former home run king and New York Yankee slugger Roger Maris.

Cleveland
INDIANS

Cleveland Indians players and fans have suffered some heartbreak when it comes to championships. In 1997 the Indians featured baseball's deepest lineup but lost the World Series in dramatic fashion in Game 7. They lost against the Chicago Cubs in 2016, once again in Game 7, this time in extra innings. Since 1948 Indians fans have been saying, "Wait till next year."

WON/LOSS RECORD:
9,191-8,837 (.510 W-L%)

HOME BASE:
Progressive Field

SUPERFACT

Many contend that Cleveland's mascot is racially offensive. In particular, Chief Wahoo, the smiling caricature illustration that has decorated Cleveland baseball attire since the 1940s, has come under scrutiny in recent years. In 2016 the franchise downgraded the Chief Wahoo logo to its secondary logo, opting for the "Block C" logo as its primary mark.

Then & Now
JIM THOME 1991–2002; 2011 / DANNY SALAZAR 2013–present

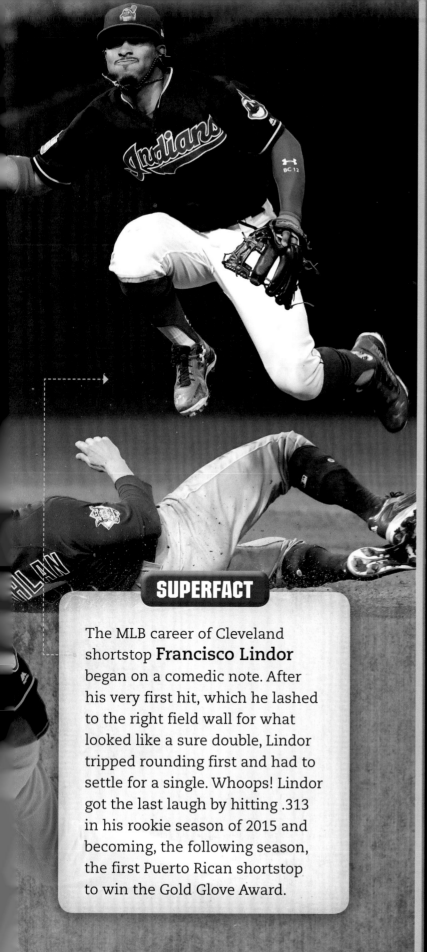

TROPHY CASE

1920, 1948

Single-season home runs:
Jim Thome, 52 (2002)

Single-season RBI:
Manny Ramirez, 165 (1999)

Single-season stolen bases:
Kenny Lofton, 75 (1996)

Career hits:
Nap Lajoie, 2,047

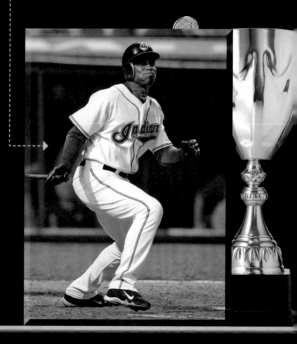

SUPERFACT

The MLB career of Cleveland shortstop **Francisco Lindor** began on a comedic note. After his very first hit, which he lashed to the right field wall for what looked like a sure double, Lindor tripped rounding first and had to settle for a single. Whoops! Lindor got the last laugh by hitting .313 in his rookie season of 2015 and becoming, the following season, the first Puerto Rican shortstop to win the Gold Glove Award.

Colorado ROCKIES

The Rockies have played in the Mile High City since 1993. Because of Denver's high altitude, fly balls tend to travel farther at the Rockies' home park, Coors Field. The Rockies used the home field to their advantage in 2007, when they reached the World Series for the first time. Their most notable player, slugger Larry Walker, was the 1997 National League MVP.

WON/LOSS RECORD:
1,784-2,042 (.466 W-L%)

HOME BASE:
Coors Field

SUPERFACT

The Rockies have a unique tradition in baseball: They hold "Purple Mondays," and don purple jerseys. Combining the colors of Red states and Blue states, the Rockies use the color purple to bring their fans together regardless of their political opinions.

Then & Now

TODD HELTON 1997–2013 / CARLOS GONZALEZ 2009–present

TROPHY CASE

Pennants:
2007 (National League)

Franchise Leaders:

Single-season home runs:
Larry Walker, 49 (1997)
Todd Helton, 49 (2001)

Single-season RBI:
Andres Galarraga, 150 (1996)

Single-season batting average:
Larry Walker, .379 (1999)

Career hits:
Todd Helton, 2,519

Career managerial wins:
Clint Hurdle, 534

SUPERFACT

Colorado third baseman **Nolan Arenado** was born in California to parents of Cuban and Puerto Rican descent. His favorite ballplayer growing up was then-Rockies star Matt Holliday. By his mid-20s, Arenado had become one of the best all-around players in baseball. He made the All-Star team in 2015 and 2016. In 2015 Arenado set an MLB record for most extra base hits in a season by a third baseman (89).

Detroit TIGERS

The Detroit Tigers are the oldest one-city franchise in the American League, an iconic franchise with roots dating back to 1901. The Tigers have won four World Series over the years but none since 1984. They did, however, recently appear in two World Series—in 2006 and 2012 under manager Jim Leyland.

WON/LOSS RECORD:
9,171-8,881 (.508 W-L%)

HOME BASE:
Comerica Park

SUPERFACT

When it comes to fashion, the Tigers keep it simple. The Old English "D" on Detroit uniforms and caps has essentially been unchanged by modern styles for more than 80 years. Their uniforms also feature more belt loops than any other team.

Then & Now
TY COBB 1905–26 / JUSTIN VERLANDER 2005–present

SUPERFACT

When Detroit acquired **Miguel Cabrera** in 2007, fans probably didn't know it would turn out to be the best trade in team history. During his decade with the Tigers, Cabrera has shown that he may be the most feared right-handed slugger of his generation, winning MVP honors in 2012 and 2013. Off the field, Cabrera started his own foundation revitalizing baseball fields and providing scholarships.

TROPHY CASE

World Series Champions:
1935, 1945, 1968, 1984

Franchise Leaders:
Single-season batting average:
Ty Cobb, .420 (1911)

Single-season home runs:
Hank Greenburg, 58 (1938)

Single-season wins:
Denny McLain, 31 (1968)

Career hits:
Ty Cobb, 3,900

Career managerial wins:
Sparky Anderson, 1,331

Houston
ASTROS

The first professional baseball games to be hosted under a domed roof happened in Houston in 1965. The Houston franchise called itself the Colt .45s from 1962 to 1964 but became the Astros in 1965. In 2013, they were shifted from the National League to the American League. Though Houston has never raised a World Series trophy, it reached the World Series in 2005, losing to the Chicago White Sox.

WON/LOSS RECORD:
4,290-4,491 (.489 W-L%)

HOME BASE:
Minute Maid Park

SUPERFACT

The Astros' most famous uniforms are the orange-and-yellow jerseys worn from the 1970s to 1993. They weren't easy on the eyes, but they sure stuck out in the crowd. Also, owing to their being the first team to play on artificial turf, the Astros are the reason the playing surface is still often called "Astroturf."

Then & Now

NOLAN RYAN 1980–88 / DALLAS KUECHEL 2012–present

SUPERFACT

Astros second baseman **Jose Altuve** was signed by Houston for just $15,000 at the tender age of 16 years old. At first, Houston declined to sign him but later reconsidered. It was money well spent: Altuve is a four-time All Star and a former Gold Glove winner. At just 5 feet 6 inches, he's also currently the shortest active player in Major League Baseball.

TROPHY CASE

Pennants:
2005 (National League)

Franchise Leaders:
Single-season batting average:
Jeff Bagwell, .368 (1994)

Single-season home runs:
Jeff Bagwell, 47 (2000)

Career hits:
Craig Biggio 3,060

Single-season ERA:
Nolan Ryan, 1.69 (1981)

Kansas City ROYALS

After winning the World Series in 1985, the Kansas City Royals went 28 seasons (1986-2013) without making the playoffs. Fueled by a mix of youngsters and veterans, the Royals made the 2014 World Series but suffered a heartbreaking home loss in Game 7. But in 2015, on the 30-year anniversary of their first title, the Royals defeated the New York Mets to become world champs again.

WON/LOSS RECORD:
3,704-3,933 (.485 W-L%)

HOME BASE:
Kauffman Stadium

SUPERFACT

In the seventh inning of a 2016 game in Detroit, the Royals found a praying mantis on top of their dugout. After players captured it by luring it onto a bat, the team gave the critter a spot in their dugout, nicknamed it "Rally Mantis Jr.," and proceeded to go on a winning streak. Sadly, Rally Mantis Jr. passed away November 2, 2016. That turned out to be exactly a year after the Royals had captured the 2015 World Series.

Then & Now

GEORGE BRETT 1973-93 / LORENZO CAIN 2011-present

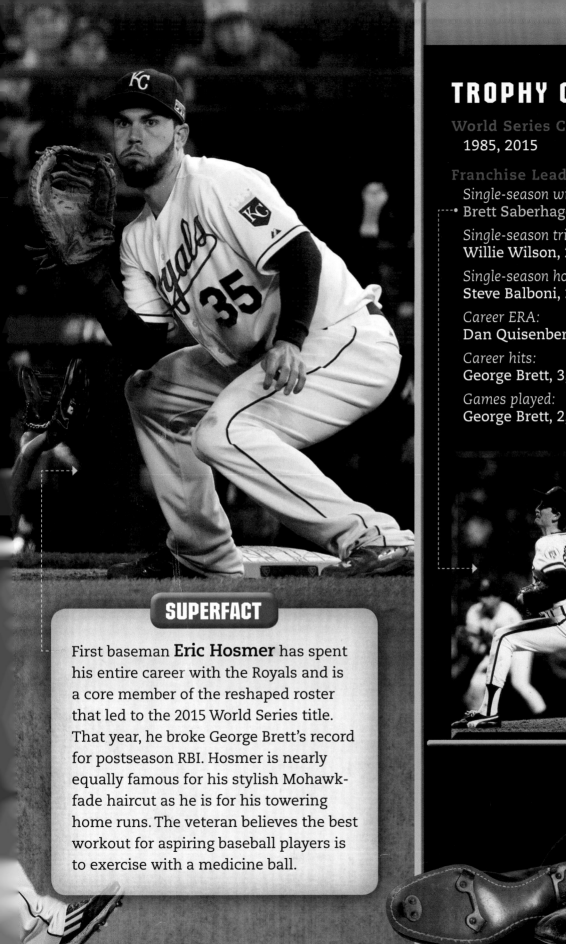

World Series Champions:
1985, 2015

Franchise Leaders:

Single-season wins:
Brett Saberhagen, 23 (1989)

Single-season triples:
Willie Wilson, 21 (1985)

Single-season home runs:
Steve Balboni, 36 (1985)

Career ERA:
Dan Quisenberry: 2.55

Career hits:
George Brett, 3,154

Games played:
George Brett, 2,707

SUPERFACT

First baseman **Eric Hosmer** has spent his entire career with the Royals and is a core member of the reshaped roster that led to the 2015 World Series title. That year, he broke George Brett's record for postseason RBI. Hosmer is nearly equally famous for his stylish Mohawk-fade haircut as he is for his towering home runs. The veteran believes the best workout for aspiring baseball players is to exercise with a medicine ball.

Los Angeles
ANGELS
of Anaheim

The Los Angeles Angels joined the major leagues as an expansion team in 1961. They were owned by Gene Autry, a movie star famous for playing roles as a singing cowboy. The team moved to Anaheim and was re-named the California Angels in 1966. In 1997 the franchise changed its name to the Anaheim Angels and won the World Series in 2002 behind third-year manager Mike Scioscia. In 2005 the team changed its name once again.

WON/LOSS RECORD:
4,477-4,465 (.501 W-L%)

HOME BASE:
Angel Stadium

SUPERFACT

The Angels were six outs away from losing in Game 6 of the 2002 World Series. Thanks in part to their unofficial mascot, the Rally Monkey, the Angels came from behind to beat the San Francisco Giants. The following night, the Angels won their first World Series in front of their home crowd in Southern California. The Angels are one of three teams, along with the Dodgers and Yankees, without an official mascot.

Then & Now
DON BAYLOR 1977–82 / ALBERT PUJOLS 2012–present

World Series Champions:
2002

Franchise Leaders:
Career batting average:
Vladimir Guerrero, .319

Career home runs:
Tim Salmon, 299

Career hits:
Garret Anderson, 2,368

Career complete games:
Nolan Ryan, 156

Career shutouts:
Nolan Ryan, 40

SUPERFACT

Angels outfielder **Mike Trout** began his minor league baseball career when he was 17 and made his Angels debut at age 19. Trout showed he belonged on the big stage from the start. He was named to the All-Star team in his first full season and won the MVP in just his third. Mike's father, Jeff, was an infielder drafted by the Minnesota Twins. Jeff Trout batted .303 over four minor league seasons but never made the bigs.

Los Angeles
DODGERS

The Los Angeles Dodgers are one of MLB's oldest franchises, dating back to 1884. They started out in Brooklyn, New York, playing that first season as the Brooklyn Atlantics. Later, they changed their name to the Grays, Bridegrooms, Superbas, Robins, and finally the Dodgers. The Dodgers moved to Los Angeles in 1958, breaking the hearts of their loyal Brooklyn fans. They franchise has won six World Series, most recently in 1988.

WON/LOSS RECORD:
10,672-9,633 (.526 W'L%)

HOME BASE:
Dodger Stadium

SUPERFACT

Though the Dodgers changed their team name a lot in the early days of the franchise, they have kept their threads the same since 1939, retaining their classic blue and white jersey style. In 1947 when Jackie Robinson became the first African-American to play in the big leagues, he dressed in Dodger blue. MLB retired Robinson's No. 42 jersey across all 30 teams in 1997. The franchise's uniforms weren't always blue, though. In 1937 they wore green.

Then & Now
JACKIE ROBINSON 1947–56 / YASIEL PUIG 2013–present

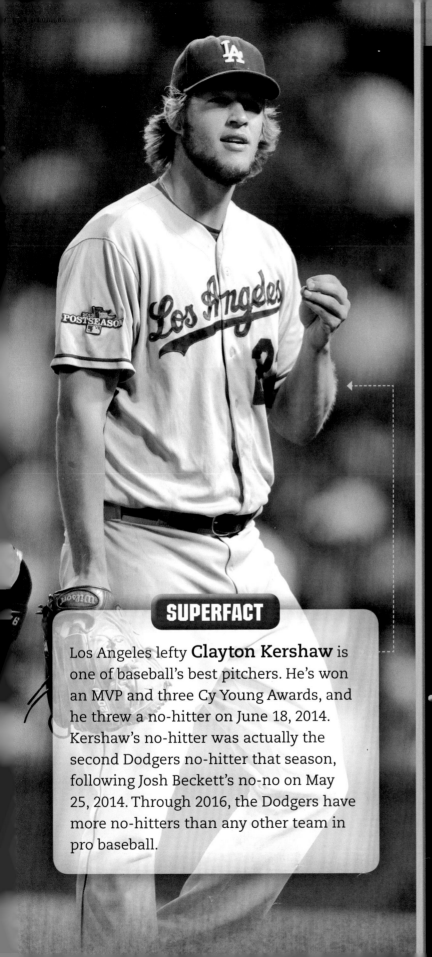

SUPERFACT

Los Angeles lefty **Clayton Kershaw** is one of baseball's best pitchers. He's won an MVP and three Cy Young Awards, and he threw a no-hitter on June 18, 2014. Kershaw's no-hitter was actually the second Dodgers no-hitter that season, following Josh Beckett's no-no on May 25, 2014. Through 2016, the Dodgers have more no-hitters than any other team in pro baseball.

TROPHY CASE

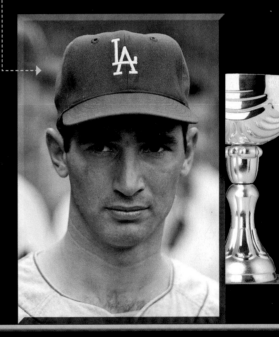

Miami MARLINS

Since their inception in 1993, the Marlins have reached the postseason only twice. But both seasons ended with World Series titles. The Marlins won the 1997 Series after coming from behind in the ninth inning of Game 7 to defeat the Cleveland Indians. In 2003 the Marlins shocked the baseball world by upsetting the mighty New York Yankees in six games to win it all again.

WON/LOSS RECORD:
1,793-2,026 (.469 W-L%)

HOME BASE:
Marlins Park

SUPERFACT

There's an unusual sight behind home plate at Marlins Park: saltwater fish tanks. The two tanks hold up to 450 gallons of water each. The team originally considered putting sharks in a tank behind the outfield wall but later reconsidered.

DONTRELLE WILLIS 2003–07 / MARCEL OZUNA 2013–present

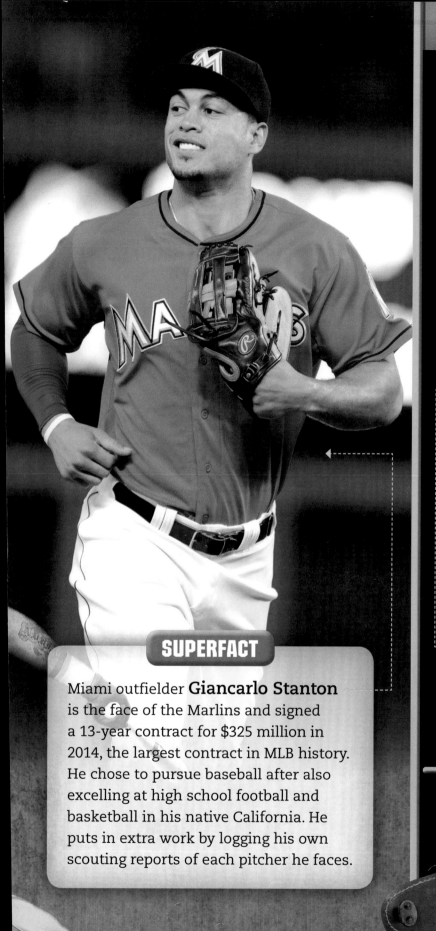

World Series Champions:
2003, 2007

2003 World Series MVP:
Josh Beckett

Franchise Leaders:
Single-season wins:
Dontrelle Willis, 22 (2005)

Single-season home runs:
Gary Sheffield, 42 (1996)

Career stolen bases:
Luis Castillo, 281

RBI in a single playoff series:
Ivan Rodriguez, 5 (2003)

SUPERFACT

Miami outfielder **Giancarlo Stanton** is the face of the Marlins and signed a 13-year contract for $325 million in 2014, the largest contract in MLB history. He chose to pursue baseball after also excelling at high school football and basketball in his native California. He puts in extra work by logging his own scouting reports of each pitcher he faces.

Milwaukee
BREWERS

After moving to Milwaukee in 1970, Hall of Famers Robin Yount and Paul Molitor helped the "Brew Crew" reach the World Series in 1982. There, they lost to St. Louis. In 1998 Milwaukee moved from the American League to the National League. They are the only team to play in four different divisions. In 2011 Milwaukee won its first division title in nearly 30 years by capturing the NL Central.

WON/LOSS RECORD:
3,642-4,001 (.477 W-L%)

HOME BASE:
Miller Park

SUPERFACT

After every Brewers home run at Miller Park, the team's mascot, Bernie the Brewer, shoots down a yellow plastic slide. Bernie is said to be loosely based on Milt Mason, a 69-year-old fan who dressed in lederhosen and vowed to live on top of the stadium's scoreboard until the Brewers drew at least 40,000 fans to a home game in the Brewers' inaugural 1970 season.

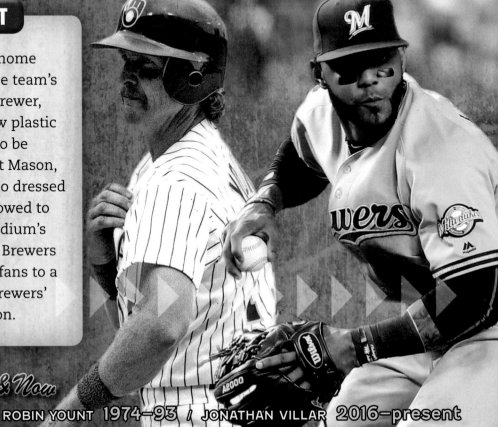

Then & Now
ROBIN YOUNT 1974–93 / JONATHAN VILLAR 2016–present

Pennants:
1982 (American League)

Franchise Leaders:

Single-season batting average:
• Paul Molitor, .353 (1987)

Single-season home runs:
Prince Fielder, 50 (2007)

Career hits:
Robin Yount, 3,142

Career RBI:
Robin Yount, 1,406

Career runs:
Robin Yount, 1,632

SUPERFACT

Brewers outfielder **Ryan Braun** has destroyed Major League pitching throughout his lengthy and successful career. The Brewers' star also enjoys pursuing interests away from the baseball diamond. He attended the University of Miami on an academic scholarship. After turning pro, he started fashion lines and opened restaurants, but baseball remained his life's passion. In 2015 Braun made his sixth All-Star team.

Minnesota
TWINS

The Washington Senators began play in 1901 and won the World Series in 1924. In 1961 the franchise moved to Minnesota to become the Twins. In the 1980s the Twins began playing at the Hubert H. Humphrey Metrodome. The loud and drafty indoor stadium helped the Twins win World Series titles in 1987 and 1991. The team has since moved outside to Target Field in Minneapolis.

WON/LOSS RECORD:
8,639-9,381 (.479 W-L%)

HOME BASE:
Target Field

SUPERFACT

The Twins' name is in reference to Minnesota's Twin Cities of Minneapolis and St. Paul. The team's original logo depicts two ball players — one on the Minneapolis portion of the Mississippi River, the other on the St. Paul side — shaking hands in friendship.

Then & Now

HARMON KILLEBREW 1954–74 / JOE MAUER 2004–present

TROPHY CASE

1924 (as Senators), 1987, 1991

Career wins:
Walter Johnson, 417

Career home runs:
Harmon Killebrew, 559

Single-season batting average:
Rod Carew, .388 (1977)

Single-season total bases:
Tony Oliva, 374 (1964)

Single-season plate appearances:
Kirby Puckett, 744 (1985)

SUPERFACT

In 2016 Twins second baseman **Brian Dozier** performed a feat that even the great Babe Ruth never accomplished: He hit 31 home runs in a 70-game span. By season's end, Dozier became the first American League second baseman to hit at least 40 homers in a season, finishing with 42.

New York
METS

The New York Mets played their first MLB season as an expansion team in 1962. They never posted a winning season until 1969, when they upset the Baltimore Orioles to win the World Series. Often relegated to being second class baseball citizens in New York due to the Yankees, the Mets added another title in 1986 and finished runner up to the Yankees in 2000 and the Royals in 2015.

WON/LOSS RECORD:
4,215-4,555 (.481 W-L%)

HOME BASE:
Citi Field

SUPERFACT

In 2012, *Forbes Magazine* named Mr. Met as the number one mascot in professional sports. Mr. Met has been a fixture at Mets games since 1964. If you have trouble finding him at a game, look for the figure with the large baseball for a head.

Then & Now
KEITH HERNANDEZ 1983–89 / YOENIS CESPEDES 2015–present

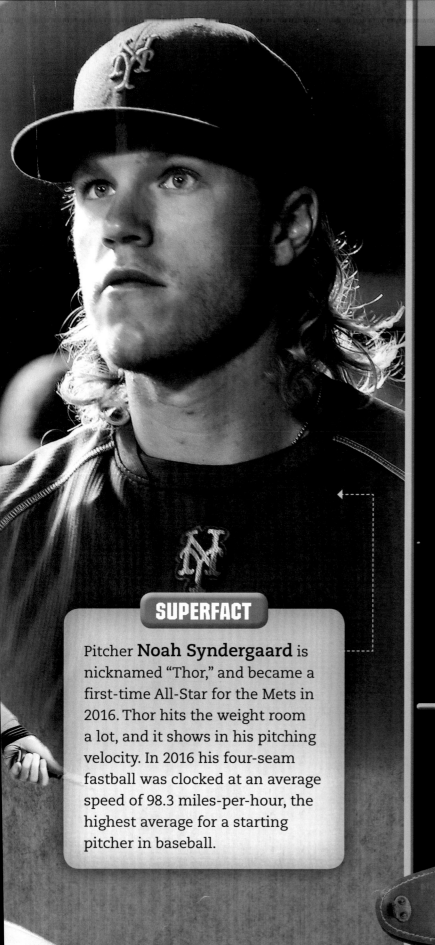

SUPERFACT

Pitcher **Noah Syndergaard** is nicknamed "Thor," and became a first-time All-Star for the Mets in 2016. Thor hits the weight room a lot, and it shows in his pitching velocity. In 2016 his four-seam fastball was clocked at an average speed of 98.3 miles-per-hour, the highest average for a starting pitcher in baseball.

TROPHY CASE

World Series Champions:
1969, 1986

Franchise Leaders:

Single-season shutouts:
Dwight Gooden, 8 (1985)

Single-season batting average:
John Olerud, .354 (1998)

Single-season RBI:
Mike Piazza, 124 (1999)
David Wright, 124 (2008)

Career home runs:
Darryl Strawberry, 252

New York
YANKEES

Love them or hate them, the New York Yankees are the kings of baseball and the most successful franchise in American professional sports. The "Bronx Bombers" have appeared in 40 World Series, most recently in 2009. Many of baseball's greatest players — including Babe Ruth, Yogi Berra, Joe DiMaggio, Lou Gehrig, Mickey Mantle, and Derek Jeter — have donned the famous Yankee pinstripes.

WON/LOSS RECORD:
10,084-7,648 (.569 W-L%)

HOME BASE:
Yankee Stadium

SUPERFACT

The famous Yankee uniform pinstripes first appeared in 1912. That means that in 2012, New York's premier baseball franchise had been wearing pinstripes on their home uniforms for a century. The team has enshrined 38 Yankees players, managers, and executives into Monument Park. Due to the Yankees keeping their pinstripes and NY logo largely unchanged, most of these figures look alike.

Then & Now

YOGI BERRA 1946–63 / AARON JUDGE 2016–present

SUPERFACT

Jacoby Ellsbury won two World Series titles with Boston before signing with the rival Yankees prior to the 2014 season. Ellsbury was a five-sport athlete in high school, and played baseball at Oregon State, where his mom filmed every game with a Super 8 camera. Ellsbury is part Navajo Native American and is the first member of the Navajo Nation to play Major League Baseball.

TROPHY CASE

1923, 1927, 1928, 1932, 1936, 1937, 1938, 1939, 1941, 1943, 1947, 1949, 1950, 1951, 1952, 1953, 1956, 1958, 1961, 1962, 1977, 1978, 1996, 1998, 1999, 2000, 2009

Franchise Leaders:

Single-season home runs:
Roger Maris, 61 (1961)

Career home runs:
Babe Ruth, 659

Career hits:
Derek Jeter, 3,465

Hits in consecutive games:
Joe DiMaggio, 56

Oakland
ATHLETICS

The Oakland Athletics, or A's, are known for their history of eclectic uniforms, unique brand of baseball, and colorful legends. In the franchise's long existence — they first played in 1901 in Philadelphia, and then Kansas City from 1955 to 1967 — the Athletics have won nine World Championships. In the 2000s, the A's reached the playoffs eight times.

WON/LOSS RECORD:
8,759-9,235 (.487 W-L%)

HOME BASE:
Oakland-Alameda County Coliseum

SUPERFACT

The mascot of the Athletics is a white elephant. In 1902 John McGraw, manager of the New York Giants, called the Athletics "The White Elephants" and meant it as an insult. But Athletics manager Connie Mack adopted the insult as a mascot, and the franchise has happily incorporated the white elephant ever since.

Then & Now
CATFISH HUNTER 1965-74 / SONNY GRAY 2013-present

TROPHY CASE

World Series champions:
1910, 1911, 1913, 1929,
1930 (as Kansas City Athletics);
1972, 1973, 1974, 1989

Franchise Leaders:
Single-season wins:
Jack Coombs, 31 (1910)
Lefty Grove, 31 (1931)

Single-season home runs:
Jimmie Foxx, 58 (1932)

Single-season stolen bases:
Rickey Henderson, 130 (1982)

Career stolen bases:
Rickey Henderson, 867

Consecutive wins in a season:
20 (A.L. record set in 2002)

SUPERFACT

When A's first baseman **Stephen Vogt** approaches the plate in his home stadium, he hears a familiar chant from the crowd. Fans start chanting, "I believe in Stephen Vogt!" Vogt has given his fans plenty to cheer about. He represented Oakland in the midsummer MLB All-Star game in both 2015 and 2016.

Philadelphia
PHILLIES

The Philadelphia Phillies are the oldest one-city franchise in American professional sports. Their roots date back to 1883, when they were called the Philadelphia Quakers. The Phillies have a rabid fan base even though the team has only won two World Series titles in its long history. After enjoying success early in the 2000s, the Phillies have been in a rebuilding phase in recent years.

WON/LOSS RECORD:
9,598-10,741 (.472 W-L%)

HOME BASE:
Citizens Bank Park

SUPERFACT

Who—or what—is that bright green thing dancing on top of the dugout during the pro baseball games in Philadelphia? Why, it's most likely the Phillie Phanatic, one of the most recognizable mascots in sports. On the team's official website, he lists his greatest moment as "the parade down Broad Street when the Phillies won the World Series in 1980 and 2008."

Then & Now
MIKE SCHMIDT 1972–89 / FREDDY GALVIS 2012–present

TROPHY CASE

World Series Champions:
1980, 2008

Franchise Leaders:

Single-season home runs:
Ryan Howard, 58 (2006)

Career home runs:
Mike Schmidt, 548

Career strikeouts:
Steve Carlton, 3,031

Hits in consecutive games:
Jimmy Rollins, 38

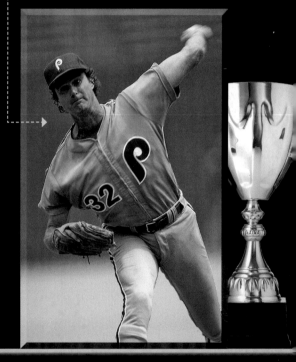

Pittsburgh
PIRATES

The Pittsburgh Pirates are one of baseball's first franchises. Their first season was in 1882, and several baseball legends have worn the Pirates 'P' — including Honus Wagner, Roberto Clemente, Willie Stargell, and Barry Bonds. After a 20-year postseason drought, the Pirates made the playoffs three straight years from 2013 through 2015.

WON/LOSS RECORD:
10,319-10,146 (.504 W-L%)

HOME BASE:
PNC Park

SUPERFACT

During Pittsburgh's 1979 World Series run, the Pirates adopted the disco hit "We Are Family" as their official theme song. In 2016 the team paid tribute to the "We Are Family"season by donning throwback uniforms from the '79 champs.

Then & Now
WILLIE STARGELL 1962–82 / STARLING MARTE 2012–present

TROPHY CASE

World Series Champions:
1909, 1925, 1960, 1971, 1979

Franchise Leaders:

Single-season home runs:
Ralph Kiner, 54 (1949)

Single-season triples:
Chief Wilson, 36 (1912)

Single-season strikeouts:
Ed Morris, 326 (1886)

Career hits:
Roberto Clemente, 3,000

Career home runs:
Willie Stargell, 475

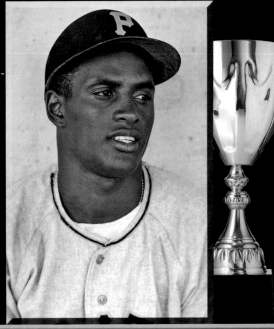

SUPERFACT

Pirates outfielder **Andrew McCutchen** was chosen by Pittsburgh with the 11th overall pick of the MLB draft in 2005. Not long after working his way to the majors in 2009, he became the standout that the Pirates had envisioned. McCutchen made his first All-Star team in 2011 and won the National League's Most Valuable Player award in 2013.

San Diego
PADRES

The San Diego Padres joined Major League Baseball in 1969. After drafting future Hall of Fame outfielder Tony Gwynn, the Padres reached their first World Series in 1984 but lost to the Tigers. Gwynn, at the twilight of his stellar Padres career, helped San Diego reach its second World Series in 1998, but the Yankees topped them.

WON/LOSS RECORD:
3,540-4,110 (.463 W-L%)

HOME BASE:
Petco Park

SUPERFACT

The San Diego Chicken may be the most famous mascot of them all. By 2015 the Chicken had made more than 5,000 appearances in nearly 1,000 different facilities. For 42 years, the Chicken has been played by one man, Ted Giannoulas.

Then & Now
STEVE GARVEY 1983—87 / YANGERVIS SOLARTE 2014—present

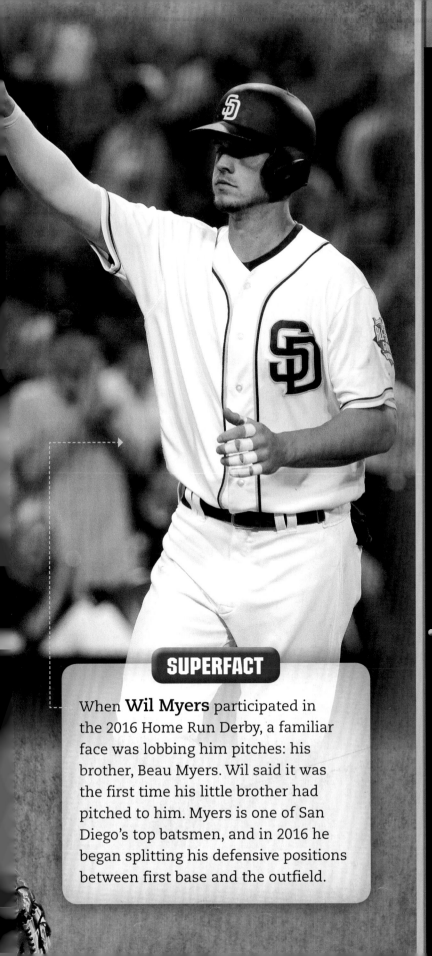

TROPHY CASE

National League Pennants:
1984, 1998

Franchise Leaders:

Single-season batting average:
Tony Gwynn, .394 (1994)

Single-season home runs:
Greg Vaughn, 50 (1998)

Career strikeouts:
Jake Peavy, 1,348

Career ERA:
Trevor Hoffman, 2.76

Career hits:
Tony Gwynn, 3,141

SUPERFACT

When **Wil Myers** participated in the 2016 Home Run Derby, a familiar face was lobbing him pitches: his brother, Beau Myers. Wil said it was the first time his little brother had pitched to him. Myers is one of San Diego's top batsmen, and in 2016 he began splitting his defensive positions between first base and the outfield.

San Francisco GIANTS

The San Francisco Giants endured a long title drought after moving from New York in 1958. But their fans' patience has been rewarded in recent years. The Giants, with a rotating cast of players, won three titles in a five-year span from 2010 to 2014. Bruce Bochy has been the team's manager for all three titles.

WON/LOSS RECORD:
10,951-9,415 (.538 W-L%)

HOME BASE:
AT&T Park

SUPERFACT

There's only about 27 feet between the sidewalk behind the right field bleachers at AT&T Park and the waters of the San Francisco Bay. It's not at all uncommon for home runs to splash down into the bay and then pop back up to the water's surface since baseballs float. The team has named the area McCovey Cove after Giants slugger Willie McCovey.

Then & Now

WILLIE MAYS 1951–72 / BUSTER POSEY 2009–present

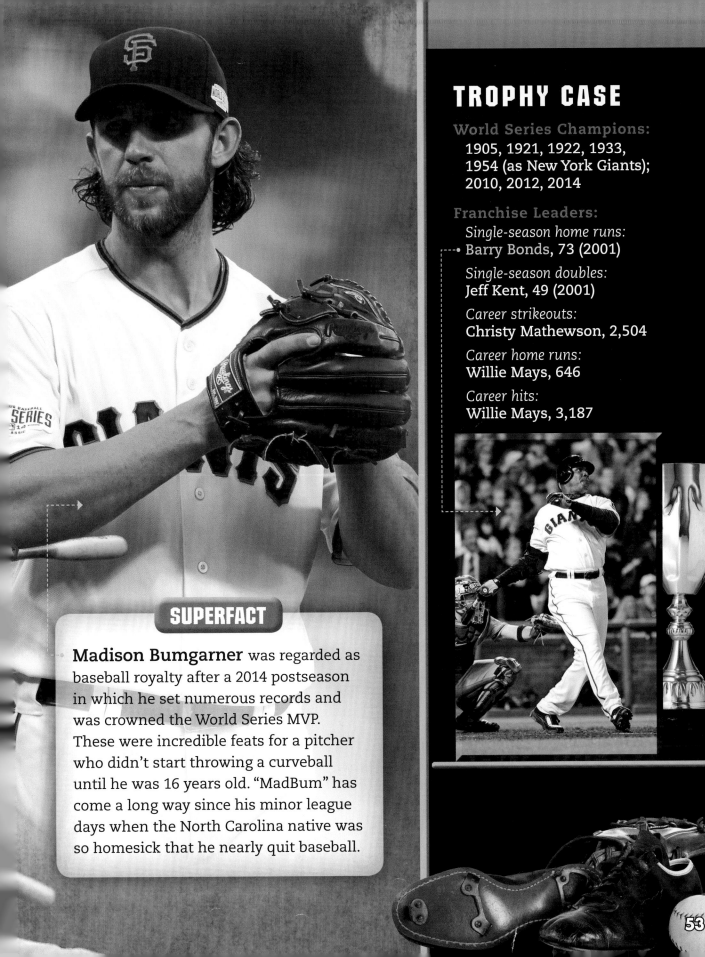

TROPHY CASE

World Series Champions:
1905, 1921, 1922, 1933, 1954 (as New York Giants); 2010, 2012, 2014

Franchise Leaders:

Single-season home runs:
Barry Bonds, 73 (2001)

Single-season doubles:
Jeff Kent, 49 (2001)

Career strikeouts:
Christy Mathewson, 2,504

Career home runs:
Willie Mays, 646

Career hits:
Willie Mays, 3,187

SUPERFACT

Madison Bumgarner was regarded as baseball royalty after a 2014 postseason in which he set numerous records and was crowned the World Series MVP. These were incredible feats for a pitcher who didn't start throwing a curveball until he was 16 years old. "MadBum" has come a long way since his minor league days when the North Carolina native was so homesick that he nearly quit baseball.

Seattle
MARINERS

The Mariners have been in Seattle since 1977. The franchise caught fire in the 1990s, when the team featured youthful superstars Ken Griffey Jr., Alex Rodriguez, Edgar Martinez, and Randy Johnson. But the team couldn't translate its talent into playoff success. After 40 full seasons, the Mariners still haven't captured World Series glory.

WON/LOSS RECORD:
2,984-3,371 (.470 W-L%)

HOME BASE:
Safeco Field

SUPERFACT

The Mariners weren't the first Major League ballclub in Seattle's history. The Seattle Pilots played at Sick's Stadium for just a single year in 1969 before the franchise moved east to Wisconsin to become the present-day Milwaukee Brewers.

Then & Now
RANDY JOHNSON 1989–98 / FELIX HERNANDEZ 2005–present

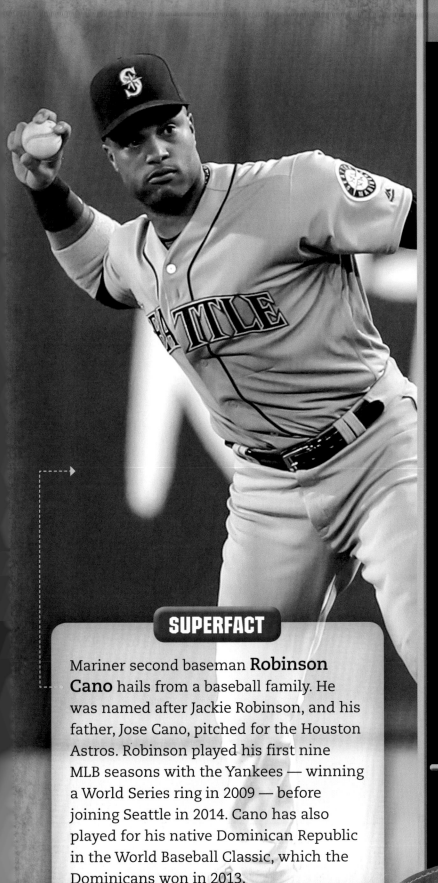

TROPHY CASE

Playoff appearances:
1995, 1997, 2000, 2001

Franchise Leaders:

Single-season ERA:
Felix Hernandez, 2.14 (2014)

Single-game strikeouts:
Randy Johnson, 19 (1997)

Single-season home runs:
Ken Griffey Jr., 56 (1997 & 1998)

Single-season batting average:
Ichiro Suzuki, .372 (2004)

Games played:
Edgar Martinez, 2,055

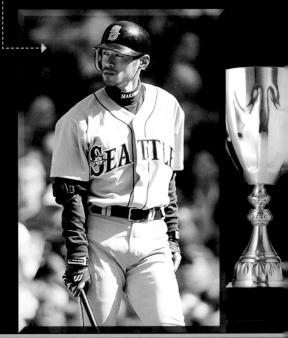

SUPERFACT

Mariner second baseman **Robinson Cano** hails from a baseball family. He was named after Jackie Robinson, and his father, Jose Cano, pitched for the Houston Astros. Robinson played his first nine MLB seasons with the Yankees — winning a World Series ring in 2009 — before joining Seattle in 2014. Cano has also played for his native Dominican Republic in the World Baseball Classic, which the Dominicans won in 2013.

St. Louis
CARDINALS

The St. Louis Cardinals are one of MLB's most decorated franchises. The Cardinals have won 11 World Series titles, the most in National League history. The Cardinals last won the Series in 2011. The Cardinals play in front of one of baseball's most passionate fan bases at Busch Stadium.

WON/LOSS RECORD:
10,657-9,839 (.520 W-L%)

HOME BASE:
Busch Stadium

SUPERFACT

During the Cardinals' 2011 playoff run, a squirrel ran across the field at Busch Stadium. Within weeks, the squirrel had its own theme song and Twitter account. Some teams have a rally monkey. That year, the Cardinals adopted the rally squirrel as their unofficial mascot.

Then & Now

STAN MUSIAL 1941–63 / KOLTEN WONG 2013–present

SUPERFACT

Cardinals utility man **Chris Carpenter** burst onto the MLB scene as a full-time player in 2012. He immediately proved his worth in St. Louis with his ability to play multiple infield and outfield positions. In 2013 Carpenter led the National League in runs and total hits and made his first All-Star team. He has recently settled in at first base but keeps his other fielding gloves handy.

TROPHY CASE

World Series Champions:
1926, 1931, 1934, 1942,
1944, 1946, 1964, 1967,
1982, 2006, 2011

Franchise Leaders:

Single-season home runs:
Mark McGwire, 70 (1998)

Single-season ERA:
Bob Gibson, 1.12 (1968)

Career stolen bases:
Lou Brock, 888

Career wins:
Bob Gibson, 251

Games played:
Stan Musial, 3,026

Tampa Bay
RAYS

Along with the Arizona Diamondbacks, the Tampa Bay Rays are MLB's youngest franchise. Born in 1998, the Rays struggled for a decade before manager Joe Maddon led a team of young prospects to a World Series runner-up finish in 2008. The Rays enjoyed six straight winning-seasons from 2008–2013.

WON/LOSS RECORD:
1,420-1,656 (.462 W-L%)

HOME BASE:
Tropicana Field

SUPERFACT

Tampa's original nickname was the Devil Rays. The team became simply "the Rays" after the 2007 season. Less must've been more; the team went to the World Series in their first season as the Rays. Addition by subtraction!

Then & Now

WADE BOGGS 1998–99 / CHRIS ARCHER 2012–present

American League Pennants:
- 2008

Franchise Leaders:

Single-season home runs:
Carlos Pena, 46 (2007)

Single-season wins:
David Price, 20 (2012)

Single-season batting average:
Jeff Keppinger, .325 (2012)

Career stolen bases:
Carl Crawford, 409

Career managerial wins:
Joe Maddon, 754

SUPERFACT

Rays third baseman **Evan Longoria** is a Tampa Bay legend. He was a rookie when the Rays made the World Series in 2008 and has been the team's starting third baseman ever since. If he weren't a pro baseball player, perhaps he would be a drummer in a rock band. Longoria is a self-taught drummer who has his own drum kit at the team's home ballpark, Tropicana Field.

Texas RANGERS

The Texas Rangers franchise moved to the Lone Star State in 1972 after spending 11 years in Washington, D.C., as the Senators. The Rangers reached the World Series in 2010 and 2011, but lost both times. In 2011 the Rangers were just a single strike away from taking the World Series versus the St. Louis Cardinals in Game 6. So close!

WON/LOSS RECORD:
4,277-4,649 (.479 W-L%)

HOME BASE:
Globe Life Park

SUPERFACT

Rangers Captain is a palomino horse, and Texas' mascot. First introduced in 2003, Rangers Captain wears number 72, a reference to the year of the franchise's relocation from Washington, D.C., to Texas.

Then & Now

NOLAN RYAN 1989–93 / YU DARVISH 2012–present

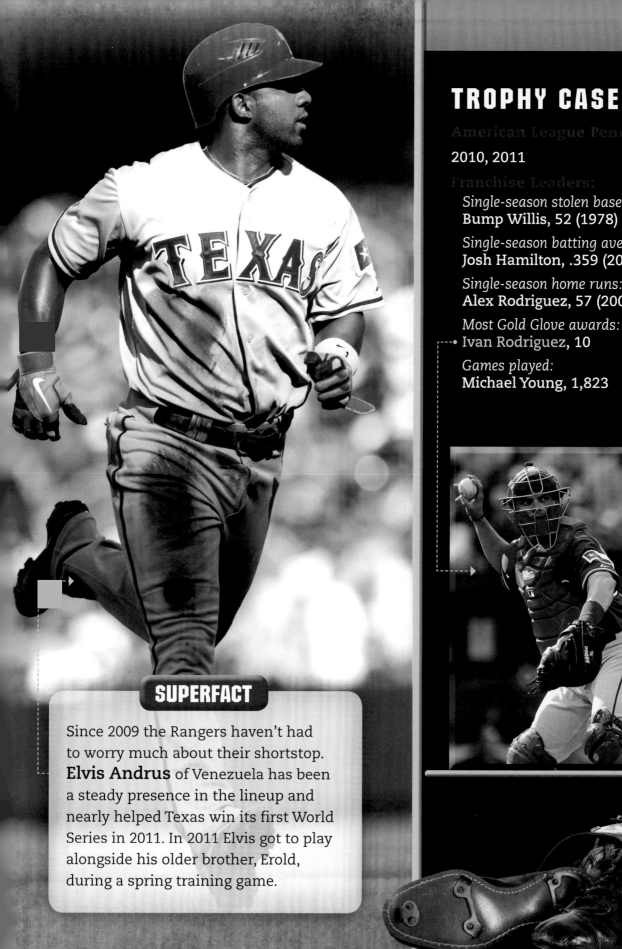

TROPHY CASE

American League Pennants:
2010, 2011

Franchise Leaders:

Single-season stolen bases:
Bump Willis, 52 (1978)

Single-season batting average:
Josh Hamilton, .359 (2010)

Single-season home runs:
Alex Rodriguez, 57 (2002)

Most Gold Glove awards:
Ivan Rodriguez, 10

Games played:
Michael Young, 1,823

SUPERFACT

Since 2009 the Rangers haven't had to worry much about their shortstop. **Elvis Andrus** of Venezuela has been a steady presence in the lineup and nearly helped Texas win its first World Series in 2011. In 2011 Elvis got to play alongside his older brother, Erold, during a spring training game.

Toronto
BLUE JAYS

In 1992 the Toronto Blue Jays became the first Canadian franchise to win the World Series. Led by future Hall of Famers Rickey Henderson and Paul Molitor, the Blue Jays repeated as champs in 1993. Joe Carter was the Series hero. His Game 6 walk-off homer at Toronto's SkyDome clinched the championship. It would be 22 years before the Blue Jays advanced to the playoffs again in 2015.

WON/LOSS RECORD:
3,167-3,188 (.498 W-L%)

HOME BASE:
Rogers Centre

SUPERFACT

The SkyDome was renamed Rogers Centre in 2005. There's a hotel in the stadium, and in 1992 the building set a World Record for most hot air balloons (46) in an enclosed space.

Then & Now

DAVE STEIB 1979–92; 1998 / JOSH DONALDSON 2015–present

TROPHY CASE

1992, 1993

Franchise Leaders:

Single-season batting average:
John Olerud, .363 (1993)

Single-season home runs:
Jose Bautista, 54 (2010)

Career home runs:
Carlos Delgado, 336

World Series MVP:
Pat Borders (1992)
Paul Molitor (1993)

Walk-off World Series home run:
Joe Carter, 1993

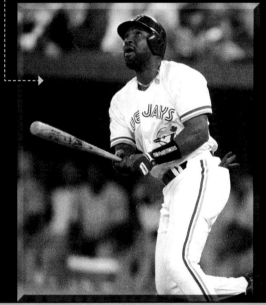

SUPERFACT

Outfielder **Jose Bautista** played for four teams before joining the Blue Jays in 2008. The rightfielder found his power-hitting stroke with the Jays and began to annually make the All-Star team, leading the league in home runs in 2010 and 2011. Off the field, Bautista established a program in his native Dominican Republic to help athletes attend college in the United States.

Washington NATIONALS

The Montreal Expos, who started play in 1969, moved to Washington, D.C., in 2005 and were renamed the Nationals. Management built a team of youngsters, and it paid off in 2012 when the "Nats" made the playoffs for the first time since their move to the nation's capital. Led by young stars like Bryce Harper and Stephen Strasburg, the Nationals also reached the playoffs in 2014 and 2016.

WON/LOSS RECORD:
3,705-3,935 (.485 W-L%)

HOME BASE:
Nationals Park

SUPERFACT

In the middle of each fourth inning at National Stadium, mascots featuring six former United States Presidents race around the field. By the end of the 2016 season, George Washington had won the race 189 times.

Then & Now
BILL LEE 1979–82 / STEPHEN STRASBURG 2010–present

TROPHY CASE

SUPERFACT

Nationals right fielder **Bryce Harper** graduated high school at 17 and made his debut in the big leagues when he was just 19. Harper made the All-Star team and was voted National League Rookie of the Year in his first season. At age 23 he became the youngest player to unanimously win the MVP. Harper credits his ironworker father, Ron Harper, for his strong work ethic.

MAPPING THE GAME

Seattle Mariners

Oakland Athletics

San Francisco Giants

Los Angeles Angels
of Anaheim

Los Angeles Dodgers

Arizona
Diamondbacks

San Diego
Padres

Colorado Rockies

Texas
Rangers

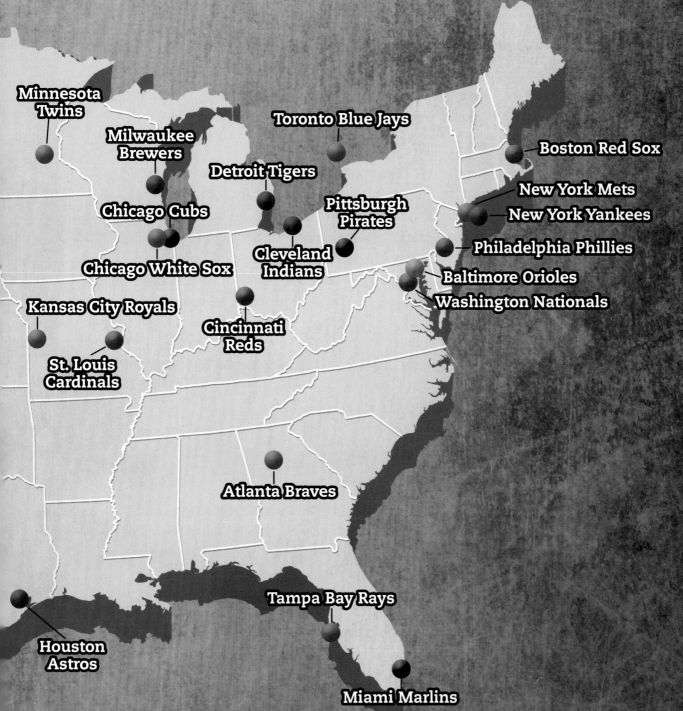

Minnesota Twins

Milwaukee Brewers

Toronto Blue Jays

Boston Red Sox

Detroit Tigers

Chicago Cubs

New York Mets

New York Yankees

Pittsburgh Pirates

Cleveland Indians

Philadelphia Phillies

Chicago White Sox

Baltimore Orioles

Washington Nationals

Kansas City Royals

Cincinnati Reds

St. Louis Cardinals

Atlanta Braves

Houston Astros

Tampa Bay Rays

Miami Marlins

TOOLS OF THE GAME

BATS

▶ The first baseball bats started appearing in the United States in the 1860s. They were made out of many different kinds of wood, including ash, willow, maple, sycamore, cherry, chestnut, and more. Ash eventually took over as the most popular wood for bats.

▶ Slugger Barry Bonds set many of his home run records in the late 1990s using bats made of maple. This created a trend of many other players switching from ash to maple wood for their bats. Though some players still use maple, the trend was short-lived. Scientific studies have shown that maple bats don't give an advantage — and Bonds was found to have used performance-enhancing drugs to gain an advantage.

BASEBALLS

▶ In baseball's earliest days in the 1840s and 1850s, pitchers often made their own baseballs. Cobblers also made early baseballs using pieces of shoe rubber, yarn, and leather for the covers. These balls were smaller, lighter, and mushier than modern baseballs.

▶ Modern baseballs are made using a cork and rubber core at the center, wound with wool and cotton, and covered in horsehide leather. Each ball has 108 stitches and is stitched by hand.

GLOVES

▶ Charles C. Waite, a first baseman from New Haven, Connecticut, was one of the first ballplayers to wear a glove. His glove was the same color as his skin. He tried to hide it because wearing it was considered unmanly.

▶ The Cincinnati Reds' Brandon Phillips won Gold Glove awards as the National League's best fielding second baseman in 2008, 2010, 2011, and 2013. He preferred that no one would ever touch his game glove. If anyone would dare to put their hand in his glove, Phillips said he'd probably fight him.

UNIFORMS

▶ When numbers first appeared on baseball uniforms, players wore numbers according to their position. Pitchers wore number one, catchers two, first basemen three, second basemen four, third basemen five, shortstops six, leftfielders seven, centerfielders eight, and rightfielders nine.

▶ Some of the very first baseball caps were made of straw. Today's major leaguers all wear a polyester cap called the "59Fifty" model made by a company called New Era. Each cap has six panels ventilated with a single hole at the top and a steel button at the cap's crown.

READ MORE

Editors of Sports Illustrated Kids. *Baseball: Then to Wow.* New York: Sports Illustrated, 2016.

Hetrick, Hans. *Baseball's Record Breakers.* North Mankato, Minn.: Capstone Press, 2017.

Kortemeier, Tom. *Pro Baseball by the Numbers.* Pro Sports by the Numbers. North Mankato, Minn.: Capstone Press, 2016.

INTERNET SITES

Use FactHound to find Internet sites related to this book.

Visit www.facthound.com

Just type in 9781515788515 and go.

CALLING ALL SUPERFANS!

Check out all of the PRO SPORTS TEAM GUIDES

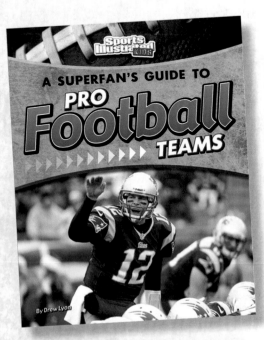

A SUPERFAN'S GUIDE TO
PRO Football TEAMS

By Drew Lyon

A SUPERFAN'S GUIDE TO
PRO Baseball TEAMS

By Drew Lyon

A SUPERFAN'S GUIDE TO
PRO Basketball TEAMS

By Tyler Omoth

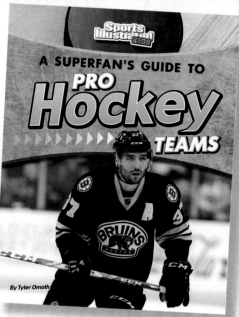

A SUPERFAN'S GUIDE TO
PRO Hockey TEAMS

By Tyler Omoth

INDEX